World Languages

Families in
Welsh

Daniel Nunn

Raintree is an imprint of Capstone Global Library Limited, a company incorporated in England and Wales having its registered office at 7 Pilgrim Street, London, EC4V 6LB – Registered company number: 6695582

To contact Raintree please phone 0845 6044371, fax + 44 (0) 1865 312263, or email: myorders@raintreepublishers.co.uk. Customers from outside the UK please telephone +44 1865 312262.

Text © Capstone Global Library Limited 2013
First published in hardback in 2013
The moral rights of the proprietor have been asserted.

Edited by Daniel Nunn, Rebecca Rissman & Sian Smith
Designed by Joanna Hinton-Malivoire
Picture research by Tracy Cummins
Production by Victoria Fitzgerald
Originated by Capstone Global Library Ltd
Printed and bound in China by Leo Paper Products Ltd

ISBN 978 1 406 25090 9
16 15 14 13 12
10 9 8 7 6 5 4 3 2 1

British Library Cataloguing in Publication Data
Nunn, Daniel.
Families in Welsh: y teuluoedd. – (World languages. Families)
1. Welsh language–Vocabulary–Pictorial works–Juvenile
literature. 2. Families–Wales–Terminology–Pictorial works–Juvenile literature.
I. Title II. Series
  491.6'681-dc23

Acknowledgements

We would like to thank the following for permission to reproduce photographs: Shutterstock pp.4 (Catalin Petolea), 5 (optimarc), 5, 6 (Petrenko Andriy), 5, 7 (Tyler Olson), 5, 8 (Andrey Shadrin), 9 (Erika Cross), 10 (Alena Brozova), 5, 11 (Maxim Petrichuk), 12 (auremar), 13 (Mika Heittola), 5, 14, 15 (Alexander Raths), 5, 16 (Samuel Borges), 17 (Vitalii Nesterchuk), 18 (pat138241), 19 (Fotokostic), 20 (Cheryl Casey), 21 (spotmatik).

Cover photographs of two women and a man reproduced with permission of Shutterstock (Yuri Arcurs). Cover photograph of a girl reproduced with permission of istockphoto (© Sean Lockes). Back cover photograph of a girl reproduced with permission of Shutterstock (Erika Cross).

We would like to thank Gareth Jones for his invaluable help in the preparation of this book.

Every effort has been made to contact copyright holders of material reproduced in this book. Any omissions will be rectified in subsequent printings if notice is given to the publisher.

Contents

Helo!

Daniel dw i.

My name is Daniel.

Dyma fy nheulu.

This is my family.

Fy mam a fy nhad

fy mam

Dyma fy mam.

This is my mother.

Dyma fy nhad.

This is my father.

Fy mrawd a fy chwaer

fy mrawd

Dyma fy mrawd.

This is my brother.

fy chwaer

Dyma fy chwaer.

This is my sister.

Fy llysfam a fy llystad

fy llysfam

Dyma fy llysfam.

This is my step-mother.

fy llystad

Dyma fy llystad.

This is my step-father.

Fy llysfrawd a fy llyschwaer

fy llysfrawd

Dyma fy llysfrawd.

This is my step-brother.

12

fy llyschwaer

Dyma fy llyschwaer.

This is my step-sister.

Fy mam-gu a fy nhad-cu

fy mam-gu

Dyma fy mam-gu.

This is my grandmother.

fy nhad-cu

Dyma fy nhad-cu.

This is my grandfather.

Fy modryb a fy ewythr

fy modryb

Dyma fy modryb.

This is my aunt.

fy ewythr

Dyma fy ewythr.

This is my uncle.

Fy nghefndryd

fy nghyfnither

Dyma fy nghefndryd.

These are my cousins.

fy nghefnder

19

Fy ffrindiau

fy ffrind

Dyma fy ffrindiau.

These are my friends.

fy ffrind

Dictionary

Welsh word	How to say it	English word
a	a	and
... dw i	do ee	my name is ... (literally: I am ...)
dyma	dumb-a	this / this is
fy	vuh	my
fy chwaer	vuh ch-why-r [2]	my sister
fy ewythr	vuh e-with-er	my uncle
fy ffrind	vuh fr-in-d	my friend
fy ffrindiau	vuh fr-india	my friends
fy llyschwaer	vuh ll-iss-ch-why-r [1][2]	my step-sister
fy llysfam	vuh ll-iss-vam [1]	my step-mother
fy llysfrawd	vuh ll-iss-v-rowed [1]	my step-brother
fy llystad	vuh ll-iss-tad [1]	my step-father
fy mam	vuh m-am	my mother
fy mam-gu	vuh m-am-gee	my grandmother

22

Welsh word	How to say it	English word
fy modryb	vuh mod-rib	my aunt
fy mrawd	vuh m-rowed	my brother
fy nghefnder	vuh ng-heaven-dare	my cousin (male)
fy nghefndryd	vuh ng-heaven-drid	my cousins
fy nghyfnither	vuh ng-h-oven-ether	my cousin (female)
fy nhad	vuh n-hard	my father
fy nhad-cu	vuh n-had-kee	my grandfather
fy nheulu	vuh n-hail-ih	my family
helo	hell-oh	hello

See words in the "How to say it" columns for a rough guide to pronunciations.

1 Note: "ll" in Welsh sounds roughly like "thl". Place your tongue as if to say "l" and hiss out of the sides of your mouth.

2 Note: In these words "ch" sounds roughly like the "ch" in the Scottish word "loch".

23

Index

Notes for parents and teachers
The spelling of words in Welsh sometimes changes, depending on how the word is used in a sentence. You may therefore find some of the words in this book spelled differently elsewhere, if seen in a different context or in isolation.